THE FOUR EMOTIONS OF
CHRISTMAS

Bob Lepine

the Four Emotions of
CHRISTMAS

10 Publishing
a division of 10 ofthose.com

Copyright © 2022 by FamilyLife.

First published in Great Britain in 2022

British Library Cataloguing in Publication Data
A record for this book is available from the British Library

ISBN: 978-1-914966-26-2

Designed by Pete Barnsley (CreativeHoot.com)

Printed in Denmark

10Publishing, a division of 10ofthose.com
Unit C, Tomlinson Road, Leyland, PR25 2DY, England

Email: info@10ofthose.com
Website: www.10ofthose.com

1 3 5 7 10 8 6 4 2

CONTENTS

WHY CHRISTMAS
MATTERS SO MUCH

Ask most adults to tell you about their childhood, and at some point, you'll likely hear a Christmas story. The impact of this particular holiday on our lives and our culture can't be overstated. Most of us carry memories of Christmases past with us throughout our lives.

For me, it's memories of growing up in suburban St Louis in the '60s. Dad bringing home boxes of Bavarian Mints. My grandparents driving down from their home in Flint, Michigan, with a case of Vernor's Ginger Ale dependably stowed in the back of their car. Singing Christmas carols door to door while collecting money for the Salvation Army. And Jell-O salad which, for some reason, only ever appeared on our dining room table at Christmas dinner.

One year, I came up with a sure-fire way to figure out if Santa Claus was real or not. I decided I would write out my Christmas list all by myself and mail it off to the North Pole without telling anyone what my list included. If I got what I wanted, he was definitely real. If I didn't, the whole elaborate ruse would be revealed. I had one big problem—I didn't know how to spell what I wanted. So I took my older sister into my confidence, enlisting her help. As I unwrapped a pair of binoculars on Christmas morning, I knew one of two things was true—either Santa was real or my sister couldn't be trusted to keep a secret!

I still remember unwrapping my first real bicycle—a Schwinn two-speed—and the ukulele I received when I was nine years old and that I still have today. We can all come up with a dozen stories of long-ago Christmases we've never forgotten. In so many ways, our Christmases as children—both the good times and the bad—shape us in ways we aren't even aware of.

CHRISTMAS SPIRIT

Each year, we expect the Christmas season to work some kind of magic on us. We go to events that will help create a "Christmas spirit". We harbor some hope that, whatever hardships or heartaches we've been through this year, the lights and carols and decorations and traditions will somehow realign our hearts and bring peace on earth, goodwill to men, and joy to the world.

Or at least, we *hope*, maybe they will bring peace and joy to us.

IN DAYS OF OLD

Christmas hasn't always been the holiday it is today. Before the birth of Jesus, the Romans used to celebrate Saturnalia in mid-December, honoring Saturn, the Roman god of agriculture. When the Roman Emperor Constantine converted to Christianity early in the fourth century, he declared that an annual Feast of the Nativity honoring the birth of Jesus would be celebrated on December 25, putting the Christian holiday at the same time as the existing pagan festivities.

WHAT'S THE REASON FOR THE SEASON?

As Christmas developed into a more secular and commercial event, Jesus became a minor part of the celebration of the season, crowded out by department store Santas, Rudolph the Red-Nosed Reindeer, Frosty the Snowman, mistletoe, eggnog, and tinsel. Christmas music starts in early November with non-stop "Rockin' Around The Christmas Tree" and "All I Want For Christmas Is You". And soon we're binge-watching all the movie classics like *Elf* or *It's A Wonderful Life*.

By the time we start humming "It's Beginning To Look A Lot Like Christmas", we find ourselves thinking more about what to get for the kids and how to decorate the cookies than about the birth of a baby 2,000 years ago.

And here's the thing—every year, along with the Christmas songs and the Christmas movies, come the Christmas emotions. Because of the oversized role the Christmas season plays in our culture and our lives, we easily find ourselves with a heightened range of emotions.

Christmas joys are deeper than other joys. So are Christmas sorrows. And Christmas stresses.

The season that promises hope and peace and joy can often bring very different, very difficult emotions. Those emotions can overwhelm us. We find ourselves wondering why the magic doesn't seem to be working for us this year. We wonder why we're feeling an emptiness instead of peace and joy and hope.

That's what this book is about. Those overwhelming emotions. Where they come from. Why we experience them as deeply as we do. And how we can learn to look past some of the trappings and clutter of the Christmas season, past those Christmas emotions—and maybe, just maybe, there's something deeper at Christmas that can bring the promised joy for which our soul longs.

1

DISAPPOINTMENT

THE BEST TIME OF YEAR?

Since I was little, I've heard Andy Williams telling me every year that the Christmas season is the most wonderful season. And Johnny Mathis comes right behind him with the assurance that Christmas will be picture-postcard perfect. It's no wonder we expect Christmas to be filled with magic and joy.

The movies tell us that too. One of my All Time Top Five Holiday Themed Movies is the original black and white version of *Miracle On 34th Street* starring worldly-wise, eight-year-old Susan. I love how her persistent cynicism is replaced by hope. Instead of rolling her eyes, she is now wide-eyed, beaming, and filled with joy—and Christmas takes on a whole new meaning for her.

As children, we grow up believing that Christmas is a magical season filled with flying reindeer, talking snowmen, and elves who live at the North Pole making toys all year round. Although we learn "the truth" as we grow up, the idea that there is something special about this time of year stays with us. We long to believe that Christmas can somehow bring us a deeper sense of joy and peace and hope. We yearn for at least *some* of the magic of the season to be real.

GROWN-UP EXPECTATIONS

Even though our grown-up expectations about Christmas have little to do with Santa and magic, they are no less real. Do any of these expectations resonate?

An expectation of happiness. We head into the Christmas period expecting that the concoction of parties and carols will lift our mood and immunize us against melancholy. There is a reason we set up holiday playlists with songs that evoke nostalgia and sentiment. It's the same reason we binge on Christmas movies, put up

Christmas lights and help ourselves to an extra spoonful of dessert. "Tis the season to be jolly," we sing. And we all expect to be jolly.

An expectation of relational harmony. The idea that everyone will get along with everyone else during the Christmas season is a set-up for disappointment. For some reason, we find ourselves imagining that any latent bitterness or hostility we're harboring will hibernate for a few weeks. We hope that maybe kindness will carry the day and that we can all agree to let bygones be bygones. But as we all know, the Christmas season is more likely to stir up relational disharmony than squash it.

An expectation of perfection. Some of us are hardwired to want things to go perfectly. The decorations must be just right. The food must look good and taste great. Every strand of lights must glow and sparkle. We even expect the climate to cooperate and give us a few inches of snow on or around December 24 so that we get our white Christmas. So, when the potatoes burn or we run out of wrapping paper late on Christmas Eve, the holiday spirit can evaporate in seconds—all because of our expectation that *this year*, everything will go just right.

But it's a myth. Anyone who has lived through a few dozen Decembers knows that a Christmas filled with happiness and harmony and everything working out perfectly is an ambition that is rarely achieved.

DISILLUSION

I expect at least one of the expectations I've outlined here has been an occasional December visitor for us. And I suspect that when reality falls short of any or all of those expectations, the season is tarnished. When our plans don't materialize as we dreamed they would, we experience disappointment, disillusionment, and loss.

Sometimes we begin to see the Christmas season as a litmus test for the whole of our lives. If we can't get the holiday season to cooperate with our expectations—delivering on happiness and bringing peace—we find ourselves thinking that nothing in life is working the way it's supposed to.

A WONDERFUL LIFE?

You may have seen the movie, *It's A Wonderful Life*. It's not by accident that it's set at Christmas time. It's a story about the frustration and disappointment we experience when our expectations are shattered and our deepest longings are unfulfilled. We meet George Bailey whose plans and dreams to go to college, to see the world, and to build skyscrapers and bridges never materialize. The "wonderful life" he envisaged was not to be and he eventually finds himself facing charges of fraud, corruption, and misappropriation of funds, leading him to contemplate suicide. Ultimately, it takes a heavenly visitation for George Bailey to recalibrate the value of his existence.

For most of us, the shattered expectations of the holiday season aren't quite as sudden or volatile as they were for George Bailey. Simple joys may bring a smile to our faces as we see one of our children performing in a concert or play, or connect with friends or co-workers at a Christmas party. But we may also find ourselves more melancholy as we read the airbrushed and edited Christmas newsletters from friends and family, and compare it with our own unedited reality.

Shattered dreams and unmet expectations are part of the human experience. They are universal. And interestingly, they show up subtly in the account of the event that Christmas commemorates—the birth of Jesus.

The biblical account of the birth of Jesus tells us that Mary and Joseph were betrothed. Couples were promised in marriage at a much younger age in those days and both Mary and Joseph were almost certainly still teenagers. Young Mary undoubtedly had dreams and expectations about being married to Joseph and beginning their new life together.

Those dreams and expectations were dashed in an instant for Mary. The Bible describes an encounter between Mary and an angel, Gabriel, who appeared with a startling message. Although she had not yet been with a man, the angel told Mary she was "with child"—the ancient way of telling her she was pregnant.

The news was just as surprising for her fiancé. Clearly, it implied that Mary must have been unfaithful to Joseph during the betrothal period. Heartbroken and betrayed, Joseph decided he had no choice but to break off the engagement. He resolved to do so quietly, to minimize the gossip and shame Mary would experience.

But Joseph had an angelic encounter of his own. In a dream, a heavenly messenger came to him, telling him to go ahead with the wedding. Mary had not been unfaithful. Her pregnancy was from God. The conception was not from another man, but from the Holy Spirit. As impossible as it sounded, his betrothed was pregnant and yet still a virgin. Joseph believed the angel, responded in faith, and ultimately took Mary as his wife.

Whatever hopes Mary and Joseph had for their wedding festivities and the start of their lives together as man and wife, the news of Mary's unexpected pregnancy forced them to have to deal with their disappointments and adjust their expectations. Apparently, disappointment and disillusionment have been part of the Christmas story from the very beginning.

DEALING WITH DISAPPOINTMENT

So what do we do when the season we've looked forward to doesn't deliver on our expectations for it? What do we do when the happiness we've counted on isn't there? What do we do when a much-anticipated reunion with loved ones isn't the joyful occasion we'd banked on?

What do we do when hidden hurts from the past resurface, leaving us isolated and alienated from one another?

How do we deal with disappointments like these?

The first step is to take a long, hard look at our expectations. Christmas movies are not real life. We don't have to begin the season in touch with our inner Eeyore—the famously gloomy and pessimistic donkey in the *Winnie The Pooh* books—but it's a good idea to temper our dreams with a healthy dose of reality.

There's nothing wrong with dreaming of a white Christmas. But when our hopes and dreams morph into expectations, requirements, demands, we're setting ourselves up for a fall. Christmas can be a special time of year—but the season does not possess some sort of magical power. We shouldn't expect it to.

Second, we need to remember that what may seem like a disaster in the moment will usually be something that we and others will look back on and laugh about for Christmases to come. *You left the sugar out of the pecan pie? You burnt the Christmas cake?* Oh well. Everyone's already had too much to eat anyway. Today's catastrophe is often tomorrow's endearing memory. It's probably not the end of the world.

Third, when it seems like everyone else is full of Christmas cheer while we are forcing a smile to hide our melancholy, it's time to redirect our thinking away from disappointments and start remembering the good things we all take for granted. That doesn't mean what we're feeling isn't valid or real. But we can choose to put that disappointment in perspective and decide not to fixate on it.

How did Jesus' mother Mary handle her disappointment when she learned that her wedding would not be happening as she had hoped? How did she process her unmet expectations? The biblical account tells us that when the angel first told Mary she was pregnant, she was confused: "How will this be?" she asked.[1] Gabriel explained that the son she was carrying was indeed special and holy and set apart for divine service. This was God's plan for her, he said.

Mary responded to the news, the disappointment, and all the shattered expectations by adjusting her perspective. "I am the servant of the Lord," she said. "Let it be to me according to your word." She moved from questioning to acceptance and chose to trust what God said to her.

Our Christmases will not all be white— but that doesn't have to ruin the celebrations. Adjusting our expectations, realizing that not everything will go perfectly, and focusing our hearts on all we have to be thankful for can help us avoid some of the disappointment.

However, even if we do manage to accept the realities of our situation, it doesn't bring ultimate peace and contentment. The feelings of serenity and satisfaction only last until the next disappointment arrives.

But maybe, just maybe, there is something about Christmas that can promise genuine fulfillment that goes on forever… Doesn't that sound like it's worth investigating?

2

STRESS

Holiday meal planning wasn't always a big deal. For our first few Christmases, Mary Ann and I just had to show up at someone else's house and enjoy the fruits of their hard work. But two things happened—children arrived and we moved house to live a long way from our families. It was a new season. We needed to establish new holiday rhythms and traditions for ourselves.

THE CURSE OF THE FAJITA

This is how fajitas became a part of our Christmas celebration.

Our neighbors in San Antonio had gradually established a Christmas Eve tradition of decorating the neighborhood with hundreds of lighted candles. It looked stunning—but it involved dozens and dozens of candles, a tower of white paper bags, and mountains of sand— not to mention several hours' work. We decided that a simple, take-out meal of fajitas and queso from the local café would be an ideal Christmas Eve family dinner. It was a bargain at less than $15 for skirt steak, tortillas, rice, beans, sour cream, guacamole, cheese dip, and chips.

In fact, it was such a success that, for the next quarter of a century, a dinner of homemade fajitas became a Christmas Eve tradition. Along the way, the menu expanded, along with the portion sizes. What began as a time-saving, bargain carry-out meal grew into a major culinary production and one of a number of not-to-be-tampered-with sacred holiday meals.

The special dinner on Christmas Eve was followed by the lovely but burdensome necessity of a special Christmas breakfast/brunch. And, of course, the special, celebratory Christmas dinner. That's a lot of kitchen stress packed into 24 hours.

It's easy to see how special holiday meals can make Christmas into a day that some people dread instead of a day they look forward to. After a few decades of tireless holiday meal planning and preparation, my wife said, "What if we skipped the fajitas this year?" I was taken aback. Violate tradition? Ruin the holiday for everyone? How could she even consider such heresy? I had no idea how much added stress our holiday meals brought to her life.

WHERE DOES IT ALL END?

And it's not just meals. There's a home to be decorated. Presents to be bought and hidden away (and then hunted for when you can't remember where you hid them). Presents to wrap. Gifts for neighbors or work colleagues to be purchased. Cards to address, the family photo shoot to schedule, and, if you're an over-achiever, the annual family newsletter to write (in September or October, of course). School functions and church functions and work functions and parties and plays. Cookies to be baked. Memories to be made. No wonder that many sensible mammals hibernate in the winter...

Add to that there's the financial stress so many people experience at Christmas. Take a look at these statistics:

- In 2021, the average American planned to spend $886 on Christmas gift giving

- Parents reported they intended to spend just short of $300 per child on presents

- Ten percent of Europeans reported going into debt to fund their Christmas shopping

- Forty percent of Americans said they expected to take on debt to buy their gifts

Debt like that equals stress. But living within our means isn't a straightforward alternative—as anyone who's dealt with disappointed kids on Christmas morning will tell you.

On top of it all, there's the relational stress. At Christmas, introverts are forced out of their comfortable nest into social obligations that leave them emotionally drained. Just the thought of crowds and parties and small talk is enough—if you add to that some already strained relationships with family members or friends, just watch what happens to your blood pressure. The thought of making conversation with people who see life differently or who want to manage your life for you is a sure-fire recipe for anxiety.

HOLIDAYS OR HOLY DAYS?

The word *holiday* was originally a reference to a religious observance. These "holy days" were designed to call people to push *Pause*, to slow down, and to commemorate some aspect of their religious faith.

Over the years, the emphasis of those holy days began to shift. People started focusing more on having a day off from work than on the event that was being observed. Spiritual commemoration gave way to the new priorities of recreation and relaxation. Before long, the word "holiday" became a synonym for taking a vacation. Even countries that are officially non-religious, like North Korea and Cuba, have holidays. A word that started off tied to spiritual devotion has been largely uncoupled from any spiritual activities. Today, a holiday is a time to take a break from the office and relax.

But who's relaxing at Christmas these days? Who is slowing down and cultivating a healthy inner life? Not many of us. Instead of "sleeping in heavenly peace", we lie awake at night thinking about everything on our plate. The holiday that is packaged as "the season to be jolly" becomes

for most of us, the season to be stressed out…
overwhelmed… exhausted.

The first Christmas brought some unexpected
stress for Mary and Joseph—not parties and
presents, but an unplanned pregnancy during
their betrothal period. Added to that, Emperor
Caesar Augustus had commanded that an
empire-wide census should be taken so he could
calculate the population. He wanted to make
sure that everyone paid their poll tax!

In practice, this meant that late in Mary's
pregnancy, the couple would have to make an 80-
to 90-mile trip from Galilee to Judea to register
with the Roman authorities. There was no mail-
in or postal vote registration available. Although
they lived in Nazareth, Mary and Joseph's
ancestors had been born in Bethlehem so, when
it came time for the census, that's where Joseph
and Mary had to go to register.

Talk about stress! Try to put yourself in their
shoes for a minute. Imagine being a pregnant
teenager, with your husband who's probably
only a year or two older, embarking on an
extended trip away from home in the middle
of your third trimester. You're more than likely
to face danger on the journey, pressure on your

finances, and long days on the road when you're heavily pregnant. And, as everyone now knows, when you arrive in Bethlehem there will be *No Vacancy* signs everywhere.

The conditions surrounding the birth of Jesus were just the beginning of a stressful season for Mary and Joseph. What they couldn't know was that before they ever made it back to Nazareth and their extended family, they would have to escape to Egypt with a young child. They would have to live as refugees for a long period while the Jewish King Herod was ordering his soldiers to put to death all of the male babies under two living in or around Bethlehem. It's hard for us to imagine what the first few years of marriage and parenting must have been like for the young couple raising their newborn son all by themselves in a foreign land.

In terms of day-to-day living, the first Christmas certainly wasn't a time of peace on earth for Mary and Joseph.

FIGHTING FOR PEACE

Fighting for peace in times of stress is not a simple task. There's no switch we can flip to turn off an anxious soul. But there are some practical steps we can take to help dial down the anxiety.

First, we can *order our priorities* for the holiday season. Author Steven Covey recommends the strategy of beginning with the end in mind.[2] When Christmas is in the rear-view mirror, the people who were part of the season with you will still be with us. People and relationships matter more than table decorations or well-ironed clothing. Secondly, we can *build some rest stops into our schedule*—by not saying "yes" to everything. Packed calendars and long to-do lists push the stress levels up. Might we be happier just scratching one or two items off the to-do list and moving on?

A third way of keeping our cortisol levels in check is to *resolve to live within our financial means*. Making a holiday spending plan before the season starts—and sticking to it. There can still be plenty of joy and memory-making when we operate on a budget. People matter more than things—it's not the price tag on our expressions of love that will be remembered. Most of us bemoan the commercialism and materialism of the Christmas season. But most of us also move right past bemoaning to shopping. "It shouldn't be this way," we say to ourselves as we pull up outside the shops or buy a couple more gifts online.

It needs to be noted here that sometimes anxiety and stress go deeper than circumstances or the pace of life. We all know people who are unable to face the circumstances of life— maybe you feel that's true of you. The idea that a few adjustments to our schedule or priorities will somehow bring the rest and peace we long for is laughable. If you're someone who faces debilitating stress and anxiety throughout the year, seeing a professional counselor or calling an organization that specializes in mental health support can be a first step toward a more manageable life.

OUT OF ALIGNMENT

For many of us, though, the extent to which the Christmas season brings stress and anxiety is a sign of how out of alignment the season has become. It's less of a holiday than ever. It's weeks of overload that require days of rest and recovery.

There are certainly ways we can dial back the stress. With some planning, some resolve, and some realignment of our priorities, we can definitely make Christmas more peaceful. But what about the stress in the days and weeks and months after Christmas? Can we ever get a grip on our stress levels?

The baby born in the manger in Bethlehem grew up and lived as a man in the midst of the pain and stress of our world—he was the one known as the Prince of Peace. History records that people laughed at him and mocked him— yet he maintained a dignified silence. He was falsely accused—yet he stayed silent. He was cruelly beaten and punished for a crime he didn't commit—yet he didn't retaliate. The Prince of Peace offers his peace to each one of us. He offers us a relationship of peace with God. A Christmas gift of immeasurable value, that lasts forever.

3

SADNESS

Do you have a worst Christmas ever? A Christmas that immediately comes to mind when you look back? Mary Ann and I do. It was our sixth Christmas together. A depressing holiday for sure.

To cut a long story short, it started in the spring when I was fired out of the blue, soon followed by the discovery that Mary Ann was pregnant. That should have been great news—but we had no regular income and only a couple of months left on our medical insurance... But then—the offer of a job! Great! But 1,000 miles away. Not so great... House on the market and long-distance relationship. Difficult times.

Eventually, we're all back together. But we don't know anyone in the new location… Mary Ann is home alone, pregnant, looking after a toddler, and sinks into depression and her well-meaning but mostly clueless husband has no idea what to do to fix it. One month later… Another job offer! This one is my dream job and for double the salary. No brainer. But now we have another house up for sale and we have to move again into an apartment near the new job.

You can imagine our emotional state as we headed for Christmas that year—our first without any friends or family nearby. Our first Christmas with just the three of us—my very pregnant wife, my three-year-old daughter, and me.

By the time Christmas morning arrived, we had just moved again. I *think* we put up a tree that year, although I have no recollection of any decorations. What I do remember is Christmas Day itself. With two mortgages and rent to pay, there was not a lot under the tree—but three-year-olds are happy ripping wrapping paper and finding hidden surprises. That took care of maybe 20 minutes.

And then... well honestly, nothing much happened. All day. Nobody stopped by because nobody knew us and we didn't know them. We hadn't yet established any festive family food traditions to add some holiday sparkle. Eating out for Christmas dinner seemed a good idea—but, pre-Internet, finding a restaurant serving Christmas dinner in a new town was challenging. We ended up at a pretty sketchy cafeteria eating what had to be the saddest Christmas meal we've ever experienced. We had nothing to do, no place to go, and no one to see.

We waited all day for the phone to ring. Surely our extended families would call to wish us a Merry Christmas and to fill us in on what was happening back home? No call... Finally, in the early evening, we called Mary Ann's family. In the background, we could hear the voices and laughter. Two minutes into the conversation, her mother said, "I'll have to call you back later—there are just too many people here. Love you." Click.

The high point of our day? Watching TV. Christmas cheer? None for us that year. It was a lonely, sad season at the end of a lonely, sad, stressful year. There wasn't much comfort or joy where we were that year—and I realize that we didn't even have it that bad.

COMFORT AND JOY?

Many of us find that Christmas intensifies the difficulties of the rest of the year. Whether it's the burden of a depressive disorder, or loneliness and isolation, or the grief of having lost a loved one—as the holiday that's supposed to be emotionally vibrant and joyful draws near, the load seems heavier. The dose of melancholy is all the harder to take in a season that is supposed to be filled with joy.

When we go to see a comedian, we go in expecting to laugh out loud. When we get tickets to a concert or a play, we attend with the expectation that we will be emotionally moved in some way. The same is true for the Christmas holiday season. We go into it expecting happiness.

"Happiness" is an interesting word. A friend once told me of an old expression: "May the happs be with you." The word *happ*, it turns out, is an old Norse term that means luck or chance. So the expression was an antiquated way of saying, "Good luck. I hope everything turns out okay for you."

Our word "happiness" incorporates the same idea. When things go well for us, we are happy. When things don't go well, we are unhappy. Our happiness is tied to what happens to us. It's all contingent on circumstances.

While happiness depends on events and circumstances, joy is something very different. Think back to Charles Dickens' classic, *A Christmas Carol*. Mean-spirited, cantankerous Ebenezer Scrooge falls asleep on Christmas Eve and, during the night, is visited by the Spirits of Christmas Past, Present, and Future. When he wakes in the morning, his outlook on life couldn't be more different: "I am as light as a feather, I am as happy as an angel, I am as merry as a schoolboy. I am as giddy as a drunken man. A merry Christmas to everybody! A happy New Year to all the world."[3]

Scrooge's circumstances had not changed while he slept. But his priorities had. For the first time in a long time, Scrooge knew joy and he found out what it was to show and experience love.

THE LOVE AND JOY OF CHRISTMAS

Interestingly, love is the central message of the original Christmas story too. The Bible points to the birth of Jesus as a statement from God telling us that we are loved. In what is probably the best-known verse in the Bible—John chapter 3, verse 16—the Bible declares:

For God so loved the world, that he gave his only Son, that whoever believes in him should not perish but have eternal life.

In the middle of what can be a bleak midwinter for many of us, it's worth stopping to ponder whether a lack of joy in our lives might be connected to a spiritual void. Might the birth of that baby 2,000 years ago be relevant to us and our emotions today?

Jesus' birth was God's love letter to the world. He is not a remote and distant God—leaving us to wallow in our messed up world. He came to earth himself as a man to show us how much he loved us. If we'd been there, we could have seen him, face-to-face. We could have watched how he brought healing to those who were sick, how he made blind people see again; we could have seen the special place he had in his heart for the dispossessed and marginalized of society.

A TIME OF DARKNESS

In the summer of 1741, British aristocrat and poet Charles Jennens and noted composer George Frederic Handel undertook an ambitious and controversial project—telling the story of the life of Jesus through words and music, but without the usual staging or scenery of operas. Jennens knew his Bible well and his libretto was made up entirely of passages from Scripture. But the oratorio caused a scandal—it was designed for use in concert halls, not churches and cathedrals. Clergy were outraged that these two men were turning the story of Jesus into a piece of popular entertainment and felt that performing it in secular venues was trivializing Scripture. Today, of course, *Messiah* and its majestic "Hallelujah Chorus" have become a beloved part of the Christmas season for many.

One of the passages that Charles Jennens selected from the Old Testament talks about darkness:

The people that walked in darkness have seen a
  great light;
and they that dwell in the land of the shadow
  of death,
upon them hath the light shined.[4]

Darkness is a wide-ranging metaphor. It can be a picture of cluelessness. If we lack information, we may say, "I'm in the dark about this." It can refer to evil or moral corruption. It's often used as a symbol of hopelessness or despair. The people the Hebrew prophet Isaiah is describing are not walking in *physical* darkness. The metaphor is a picture of barrenness, emptiness, and hopelessness. He is describing a dispirited nation, stumbling through life without focus or purpose or hope. They were living "in the land of the shadow of death" and had nothing to live for.

That's similar to how some people feel during the Christmas season. They feel like they are walking through life in a cloud. Life is a misery. They find themselves in darkness, asking over and over again, "What's the use?"

Have you experienced that kind of despair in your own heart? Many people do. While there may be a biological source of our depression that may need medication or professional help, it may also be connected to our circumstances. The holiday season can reveal fractures in our relationships with one another. It can bring to the surface unhappinesses that have remained hidden for years. We can find ourselves hit with waves of sadness that wash over. And we feel helpless to push back on the darkness we're feeling.

STRATEGIES FOR SADNESS

Here are a handful of strategies that counselors and mental health professionals recommend for tackling sadness:

Practicing intentional gratitude—making a list of five things which we're thankful for, every day—running water, dependable electricity, socks, enough to eat, a friendly smile.

Scheduling time for rest in a relentless season. The Bible would remind us that God rested on the seventh day. He was onto something there!

Volunteering. Sounds crazy? Having a positive impact on the lives of other people can bring us comfort and joy at the same time.

Being smart about alcohol. It may boost our mood short-term, but it's a depressant. Drinking too much doesn't drown our sorrows, it increases them.

Eating right and getting plenty of sleep and exercise. You knew this was coming, right? Good food, sleep, and exercise *do* make a difference.

Spending time with people who care. Isolation and loneliness are accelerants when it comes to sadness and depression. It may be a good idea to take the initiative to link up with friends?

A PERMANENT SOLUTION?

I hope you'll find that one or two of those strategies will chase away some of the Christmas blues. But, as helpful as they may be, they'll never achieve permanent happiness for us. Something more than a change of habits, or doing something helpful for others is needed— something deep; something lasting; something supernatural. Is permanent happiness even possible? I think it is...

Centuries ago, a church bishop in North Africa famously observed that our hearts are restless until they find their rest in God. Is your heart restless? The thing that brings real contentment, peace, and joy to our lives is when we have a deep sense of belonging and connection. You've probably met people who seem to have a reservoir of strength that helps them keep from crashing when life gets hard. A lot of those people would tell you that their source of strength is the connection they have with God. Christmas is a perfect time to consider whether there is a missing connection to God in our lives.

In the end, the only solution for darkness is light. That's what happened, according to the prophet Isaiah. Light came to the people who were living in the land of the shadow of death and the light brought them out of their darkness. It was a great light.

LIGHT OF THE WORLD

Like most Christians, when Charles Jennens looked in the Bible, he was convinced that the light that Isaiah was talking about was ultimately revealed 700 years later. The light Isaiah saw shining in darkness was looking forward to the time when Jesus would be born. Later in the Bible, we come across the familiar account of a bright star that lit the path for the Magi who came to pay tribute to the child they believed was a newborn king. Jesus is spoken of as "the true light who gives light to everyone." And history records that Jesus declared himself to be "the light of the world." Quite a claim. Do you think it could be true?

Don't you think it's extraordinary that people still talk about a baby who was born over 2,000 years ago? There is something undoubtably different about this baby. Something that splits history in two—BC and AD. Something that means the world stops every year to celebrate, remembering his birth into this world. Might it be possible that he was right to call himself "the light of the world"? Might it be possible that he has something to teach us about where to find happiness?

Look at what history tells us about his life and his character, about what he said and did. One of Jesus' friends—someone who knew him well—said that nothing bad ever came out of his mouth. Imagine that! Most of us only last an hour or two—or maybe a moment or two— before something selfish pops into our head or out of our mouth. But Jesus brought light. He was totally pure. Totally brilliant. He lived a life that none of us could ever live. He told people how they could have a relationship with the living God. More than that, he made a way for it to be possible. By his death he carried on himself the sins of the world, and gave humanity the way to be right with God and have life, full life, today and forever. He wants to share his light with us. It almost sounds too good to be true doesn't it? But this is a reality that you can have…

4

JOY

I don't know how much you've thought about emotions—what they are, where they come from, whether they control you or you control them. Those kinds of questions have been spinning through the minds of philosophers, psychologists, and psychiatrists for eons. Or at least for as long as there have been philosophers, psychologists, and psychiatrists.

WHAT ARE YOU DOING HERE?

Emotions are typically uninvited guests. They just show up. Sometimes we're happy to see them. Sometimes we wonder, "Why did you have to drop in now?!" Sometimes we intentionally seek to stimulate certain emotions, like when we choose a particular movie to watch. Do we want a comedy? Something scary? Something sad? We pick our movies based on the emotion we're hoping to arouse.

The simplest definition of emotion is "a strong feeling". The American Psychological Association goes a little deeper and defines an emotion as "a complex reaction pattern, involving experiential, behavioral, and physiological elements, by which an individual attempts to deal with a personally significant matter or event."[5]

DEALING WITH BEARS

Dr Bill Gillham, who taught psychology to college students for years, liked to explain emotions this way. All of us, he said, navigate life using our mind, our will, and our emotions—or as he liked to say, "our thinker, our doer, and our feeler."[6] We respond to whatever we experience based on what our brain tells us and what our heart tells us.

He used this illustration. Imagine you're walking in the forest one day when you see a grizzly bear. Your "thinker" immediately tells you that bears live in Yellowstone National Park and come into campgrounds foraging for food, that bears eat people—and you are a person.

Those facts register in your "feeler"—and you immediately respond with fear, anxiety, dread, and panic. In a millisecond, you have switched from feeling serene and peaceful to intensely fearful. And that's a good thing—you should be afraid.

The combination of what you're thinking and what you're feeling lands at the doorstep of your "doer"—your will—and determines how you respond. In this case, your doer responds to the bear by opting to run in the opposite direction.

But suddenly you are reminded of the article you read on the National Park website before starting on your hike. According to the US National Park Service, if a bear starts paying attention to you, the right response is to start talking calmly to it. True fact! Let the bear know you're a human. Stay still. Stand your ground. Slowly wave your arms. Stay calm. No high-pitched squeals. And definitely no screams or sudden movements.

But *knowing* the right thing to do and *doing* the right thing are not always the same. You might know that it's better not to run—but your emotions don't care! They are telling you to get out of there fast. That bear might have been looking for picnic baskets, but now that he's found you, he may decide to come at you any minute.

THE BATTLE

It's so often the battle between what we *think* and how we *feel* about things that gets us in trouble. The problem is, while our emotions are real and important and valid, they are unreliable. Of course, our emotions should not be dismissed or disregarded. We have them for a reason. But when our emotions want to overrule what we know is true or right or wise, we have to learn how to manage them properly. It's one mark of maturity. Two-year-olds have no idea how to manage their emotions and, as a result, the rest of us get to experience *the terrible twos*. Part of growing up is learning how to control our emotions and to override them when necessary.

Long-time fans of the Star Trek TV and movie franchise are familiar with Mr Spock, with his mixed human / Vulcan heritage. Spock famously responds to all stimulus with reason and logic. When he witnesses an emotional response from a member of the crew, he will most often raise an eyebrow and declare the display of human emotion as "highly illogical". Under pressure, Spock is unnerved. He doesn't get fearful or flustered. But he also doesn't experience joy or love. While viewers see the obvious value in his clear-eyed approach to life, we also see that the absence of emotion robs him of the full experience of humanity.

Our goal with our emotions is not to become like Mr Spock. He would probably have no problem standing his ground if he saw a bear in the woods, because it would be the logical thing to do. And he might be able to get through the Christmas season without having to deal with stress or disappointments or sadness.

But you know what he'd miss, don't you? He'd miss what all of us long to experience during the Christmas season. He'd miss the joy. The hope. The excitement. The love. He would have none of these wonderful uninvited guests dropping in on him, enriching his holiday. As a result, his Christmas would be like any other day.

How sad that would be. And we all know that Christmas is supposed to be a time for being merry!

MERRY GENTLEMEN

There is really only one time of year when the word merry becomes a regular part of our vocabulary. We don't wish our neighbors a "Merry Fourth of July". No one says to his or her sweetheart, "Merry Valentine's Day". In the twenty-first century, if someone says the word "merry" we know what comes next. It's either "Christmas" or "go-round".

The word "merry" means "high spirited". When you wish someone a Merry Christmas, that's what you're hoping for them—a holiday season where spirits are high, where stress and sadness are kept at bay, and expectations aren't over inflated. In our mind, *merry* and *Christmas* go hand in hand. They belong together. But what we all long for is not just a few days of merriment… but a deep-seated, long-lasting merriment that comes from something, *someone*, beyond the decorations, our circumstances, and the festivities.

No one knows who wrote the lyrics of the familiar carol, "God Rest Ye Merry Gentlemen", which dates back more than five centuries, but did you know that there's actually a comma in the title? In fact, it is a matter of scholarly debate![7] But perhaps you're not into the niceties of punctuation—so let me summarize by saying that the carol isn't talking about "merry gentlemen" getting a good rest, but expressing a desire that God would allow the gentlemen to "rest" or remain merry.

> *God rest ye merry, gentlemen*
> *Let nothing you dismay.*

And the reason for merry hearts and the absence of dismay at Christmas? It's this:

> *Remember Christ our Savior*
> *Was born on Christmas Day;*
> *To save us all from Satan's pow'r*
> *When we were gone astray.*

> *O tidings of comfort and joy, comfort and joy,*
> *O tidings of comfort and joy.*

The "merriness" of Christmas is wrapped up in remembering that "Christ our Savior was born on Christmas Day" and that the purpose of his birth was "to save us all from Satan's power when we were gone astray". Those are the "tidings of comfort and joy". Let's try and unpack that a bit…

ALL I WANT FOR CHRISTMAS

No one wants a Christmas season marked by disappointment, stress, and sadness. We expect the holiday to live up to its promises of joy, peace, happiness, and love. Something deep inside is hoping and longing for Christmas to fill up what is empty in us.

Behind the mythology and traditions of Christmas is a true story. An historical event. A real human baby was born in the little town of Bethlehem, on the outskirts of Jerusalem. At the time of his birth, only a handful of people had any idea that something significant was happening—just his teenage parents who had been tipped off by an angel; a handful of working men looking after the sheep, confronted by a sky full of angels telling them to look for the child in a nearby stable; and the wise men, the Magi, who saw the star. But that's it. No one else knew that anything special was happening.

But it certainly was special. This birth had been anticipated and prophesied about for centuries. Angels don't usually show up at the birth of a child. But the angels and the prophets knew that this baby was one promised by God. The long-awaited one. The one who would one day rule in peace and justice and righteousness.

There is an interesting and often neglected story about the birth of Jesus that points us back to the true source of Christmas joy. It's found in chapter two of the Gospel of Luke. It's about an old man named Simeon and the time he met the infant Jesus.

The Jewish Law required Joseph and Mary to go the temple to make a sacrifice to mark the birth of their firstborn son. As they entered the temple courtyard, they found themselves face-to-face with an old man—tradition says Simeon was 113 years old. He was a devout and pious Jew, and went to the temple each day to pray.

Somewhere in his past, Simeon had received a promise from God. The old man had been waiting for God to send the longed-for Messiah to deliver the nation from its enemies and bring peace and prosperity—the kind of peace and prosperity the Jews had known centuries earlier. Simeon believed that God had promised that he would not die before this Messiah came. So, every day, he went to the temple courtyard. And every day, he prayed that this day might be the day that the promise would be fulfilled.

As Mary and Joseph entered the courtyard, something stirred in Simeon's soul. He approached the young couple, feeling sure this child, out of all the children being brought to the temple each day, was the promised one, the one who would bring "consolation" and comfort to God's people, in fulfillment of the Hebrew Scriptures.

Imagine being a young couple with a new baby in your arms, being approached by a 113-year-old man who asks you if he can say a blessing over your child. That's what happened to Mary and Joseph. Maybe they wondered if this old man was crazy. But they handed their son to Simeon, who took him in his arms and blessed him.

"Lord," Simeon said, "I can now die in peace because, just as you promised me, I have seen your salvation in this child. This boy will grow up to be a light who points the way for people to come to believe in you and worship you."

Seeing Jesus and realizing how significant this child was brought deep joy and peace and hope to the heart of this old man that day. Simeon knew in the depths of his being that this child had been sent by God for a specific purpose. The prophets had promised that the light of God would shine in a land that was filled with darkness. And finally, the long-awaited King had been born. He would grow up to rule and reign over a kingdom that would be characterized by peace and joy and love. A kingdom where even lions and lambs would lie down together, and where swords would be turned into farming implements because wars would cease.

MISTAKEN?

Anyone checking today's headlines would have to conclude that Simeon was sadly mistaken about the identity of Jesus. Simeon believed that this baby would be the one who would bring peace and hope and joy into the world—but the world is full of war and strife. What's more, just three decades after this incident in the temple, Jesus' mother watched as her son was charged with treason and nailed to a Roman cross. That wasn't the outcome that the old man in the temple had prophesied for her son, was it?

But, as Mary watched Jesus being crucified, she would have recalled something else the old man had told her. Simeon had said to Mary: "this child will bring about the fall and rising of many in Israel. He will face opposition. Because of him, the thoughts of many hearts will be revealed. And you, Mary, will experience profound pain and grief. A sword will pierce your own soul."

They had been cryptic words at the time Simeon said them. Now, as Mary watched her son being crucified, this part of the old man's prophecy was coming true.

Simeon was right. God had sent a King who would bring salvation to the whole world—but it wasn't to do with restoring the glory of the Jewish empire. God had sent a King who would usher in a new kingdom, but it was a kingdom that was "not of this world".

HIS BIRTH AND HIS DEATH

Our favorite Christmas carols point to the birth of Jesus as the source of peace and hope and joy. But we have to look beyond his birth to understand how we can experience that peace and hope and joy for ourselves. Ironically, it is to Jesus' death that Christians ultimately look. It wasn't his coming that mattered most. It was what he accomplished when he came, when he died, and when he rose again.

The key to finding the peace and hope and joy and love we long for all year long—but especially at Christmas—is wrapped up in believing and trusting that the person whose birth is being celebrated really is who he claimed to be. Believing that he truly is the God of the universe, who came to live among us as one of us, fully human and yet still fully God. It's when we recognize that the one who created us came to establish a relationship with us that we start to see the ultimate meaning and purpose for our lives.

THE HEART
OF CHRISTMAS

In this book, I've offered practical ways to help us deal with the disappointments, the stress, and the sadness that can be part of the Christmas season. But those practical ideas are just band aids or plasters. They are aspirin. They can help address the symptoms a bit—but they don't offer a real cure. In our heart of hearts, we know that. For the Christmas season and the rest of life to be what we long for it to be requires a fundamental realignment of our lives around a new center. It involves nothing less than embracing an essential understanding of the significance of the very first Christmas.

The reason God came to walk among us as one of us, as a human being, was to call us into a relationship with him. We only find the love he knows we're longing for, the hope we need, the joy we seek, and the peace that so often eludes us when our lives are reoriented from our self-focused, self-serving, self-absorbed mindset to a new way of living. According to the Bible, our lives don't just need a minor adjustment. We need a whole new life. And that's the gift Jesus came to bring us. A new life with him at the center.

Here's how we receive this gift.

TURNING

First, we own up to the fact that our lives are not what they should be. We live in a world that is broken. And we see that brokenness in our own lives as well. When we're honest, we realize that the more we try to take control, the more of a mess things become. Even if we find success or achievement in one area of our lives, other areas fall far short.

The Bible has an explanation for why we experience this brokenness in our lives and in our world. It's because we have disregarded

God and taken matters into our own hands. It's like we've drawn a circle around our lives and declared ourselves "lord of the ring". We might call out to God when things get tough, but for the most part, we resist having anyone else calling the shots.

The word the Bible uses to sum up this self-oriented way of living is *sin*. We tend to think of sin as a collection of bad habits or human failings. But those bad habits or human weaknesses are the manifestations of the central issue: our rejection of God. Pride, self-centeredness, and unbelief are the root cause of all that is wrong about our lives and our world—thinking that we can run things ourselves, without God. According to the Bible, "all have sinned and fall short of the glory of God". Before we can have the new life Jesus offers us, we have to settle in our own hearts that trying to take control and run our own lives doesn't work out well for us.

The Bible also tells us that there is a penalty for rejecting or ignoring God. The message is very stark. Rejecting God brings judgment and death. It puts the joy and peace and love we long for eternally out of reach. Instead, the anguish and unrest we've tasted in this life will be ours forever. "The wages of sin is death," the Bible says, "but the free gift of God is eternal life in Christ Jesus our Lord."

COME, FOLLOW ME

In his death on the cross, Jesus Christ took on himself the pain and the penalty we deserve. The Bible says he bore our sins and our sorrows and that "God shows his love for us in that while we were still sinners, Christ died for us". Jesus stood in our place and received the judgment we deserve for having rejected God. Because of his death, when we turn to him and pledge our allegiance to him, our sins are forgiven and we get a clean sheet. The old things pass away. New things come.

The resurrection of Jesus is the defining moment in all of human history. Not only does it resolve the mystery of whether there is life after death, it removes the threat of what the Bible refers to as "our final enemy"—in other words, death. Who else has risen from the dead? No one empties a grave like Jesus! He referred to himself as "the resurrection and the life"—and left an empty tomb to prove it! When we turn away from a self-directed life and surrender to

Jesus, the Bible says that the same Spirit who raised Jesus from death comes to dwell in us.

That's the second step in receiving the gift of new life. We turn from our self-oriented life to a new God-centered, God-directed life. We decide to turn over control of our lives to Jesus, and follow him as our King and Master. He says "if anyone would come after me, let him … follow me". To receive his gift of new life, we respond by saying "I'm in. You lead. I'll follow."

A NEW HEART

When we take those two steps—turning from our sin and following Jesus—he gives us a new heart. A new purpose for living. A whole new life. And along with that new life comes the peace, the joy, the hope, and the love for which our soul longs. Not just at Christmas. But all year long.

This doesn't mean there'll be no more hardship. No more sadness. No more disappointments. No more stress. Anyone who tries to tell us that life can be perfect is probably trying to sell us something. But, if we're following Jesus, it means that when hardship or sorrow or frustration or anxiety come our way, we will not face these challenges alone. Our new life means we have new resources at our disposal. We have a God who is for us and will never abandon us when life gets hard. "Cast your cares on me," he says. "Bring your burdens here. Find what your soul is looking for as you walk each day with me."

This is the Christmas gift Jesus came to earth to bring. The key to finding the joy and love and hope and peace that Christmas promises is coming face-to-face with the person whose birth we celebrate and choosing to receive the new life he offers.

As you come to the end of this book, maybe you're thinking you're ready for your life to change and that you would like to start a new life with God. Maybe the promise of fulfilment, peace, happiness, and joy forever resonates in your heart. If someone gave you this book, why not talk to them about it and maybe go to their church with them to hear more from the Bible about Jesus? Or perhaps you might like to look at an explanation of the gospel online on a website like Christianity Explored.[8]

But maybe you're clear that you want to accept God's gift of forgiveness right now. You can do that by praying to him, using your own words. Tell him that you want to stop running your own life and turn back to him, tell him that you want to follow him from now on.

When you pray that prayer with a sincere heart and begin living out your new life by following Jesus—Jesus promises that you are "born again". God forgives you your sin and welcomes you into an everlasting relationship with him. Just like any newborn, you're going to need the help of others to grow. A great place to begin is in a local Christian church. Again, if someone gave you this book as a gift at Christmas, it's very likely that they are already a part of a local church. They would love to hear about your desire to follow Jesus. And they'd love to have you attend a church service with them and talk with you about having a new life in Christ.

In December 1865, a man called Phillip Brooks had a fresh reminder of the real meaning of Christmas. Brooks was the long-time Rector at Boston's Trinity Church, and in the winter of that year, he decided to go on a pilgrimage to Jerusalem. In those days a trip from Boston to Israel was a significant endeavor and being in Israel at Christmas-time had been a lifelong dream for him. On Christmas Eve, he traveled on horseback from Jerusalem to Bethlehem which is around six miles to the south. Before dark, he and his companions rode out into the nearby fields where the shepherds would have experienced the angelic visitation. He was surprised that centuries later, the Judean hillside was still populated with shepherds who were keeping watch over their flocks.

That night, Brooks led a Christmas Eve worship service at the ancient basilica built over the traditional site of the nativity. The service began at 10 pm and lasted until 3 am on Christmas morning. With his heart full from reflecting on the birth of Jesus, Brooks began to write the words to a carol we still sing today:

O little town of Bethlehem, how still we see thee lie…

His final verse for that familiar carol sums up for us the promise of Christmas:

O holy Child of Bethlehem, descend to us we pray;

Cast out our sin and enter in, be born in us today;
We hear the Christmas angels, their great glad
    tidings tell;
O come to us, abide with us, our Lord, Emmanuel.

It is knowing that holy Child of Bethlehem for ourselves, asking him to cast out our sin and come into our lives that makes sense of Christmas—and makes sense of life. It is receiving new life from him that replaces disappointment, stress, and sadness with true and lasting joy and peace.

You can know his joy, his peace, and his love this Christmas. You can know it today. Jesus promises that when we ask, he loves to give. We can come to him, saying sorry for the ways we've ignored and rejected him, turning from that and receive the forgiveness he offers—and we can do that today! The stresses and emotions of Christmas can be put into perspective as we experience the first taste of happiness and peace that will last forever.

With all my heart, I wish you a very Merry Christmas! A Christmas of joy and peace and love.

ENDNOTES

1 You can read about it in the Bible in Luke chapter 1, verses 26–38.

2 This is Habit #2 in Steven Covey's book *The Seven Habits of Highly Effective People* (New York, Free Press, 2004).

3 Charles Dickens, *A Christmas Carol* (1843).

4 Aria from Handel's *Messiah*, based on Isaiah chapter 9, verse 2.

5 https://dictionary.apa.org/emotion

6 This is drawn from Dr Gillham's book, *Lifetime Guarantee* (Harvest House Publishers, Eugene OR, 2012).

7   If you'd like to know more about this
    debate, see https://www.latimes.com/
    opinion/letters-to-the-editor/story/
    2021-12-25/dont-forget-the-comma-in-god-
    rest-ye-merry-gentlemen

8   https://www.christianityexplored.org

10 Publishing